Lines, Rhymes and Whimsical Poems

Gail Frye Winter

authorHOUSE®

AuthorHouse™
1663 Liberty Drive
Bloomington, IN 47403
www.authorhouse.com
Phone: 1 (800) 839-8640

Published by AuthorHouse 08/28/2015

ISBN: 978-1-5049-3460-2 (sc)
ISBN: 978-1-5049-3461-9 (e)

Contents

Give Me a Noun and I'll Make You a Rhyme

Just For Students

Nature

Winter

For Family and All The Memories

Sunday School Poems

Foreword

My love for poetry began early in my life as I would listen to my grandmother, Gertrude Neal, recite "Twas the Night Before Christmas" every holiday season. She knew it by heart and was very animated as she made the poem magical. She also did "Lil Orphan Annie" with the same flair, and I loved the lilt and rhythmn in her voice and the sing song of the rhyme. I was amazed that she could do this by heart. I knew then that I loved poetry. This love continued as I grew and read to my own children.

I became a teacher of Language Arts and found that writing poetry and teaching poetry was dear to me. Most of my students seemed to have a dislike for poetry and a fear of attempting to write any of their own. One day, as I was trying to peak their interest in a little composing of their own, with which they were showing little interest, I challenged them to give me a noun, any noun, and I would attempt to write a little "ditty" off the cuff. Nouns came flying my way. At last, I had their interest. Thus began my writing of poetry. Many of these "off the cuff" poems are included in this book. You will notice they are the ones with a single noun title.

Some of my happiest poems are those written for special occasions. This began in a most unexpected way. At my nephew's birthday I was found lacking a birthday card. As I dug through my potpourri of stationary, I found a blank card with a bluebird on the front. Thus began my Bluebird poems. For birthdays, graduations, new babies, and other important events a Bluebird poem was composed through Bluebird's eyes. It was so much fun to put those special things, known only for that special person, in rhyme. I have put a few of those in this book also. Although they may not mean so much to the reader, they meant much to whom they were sent.

Working with children in church gave me the opportunity and pleasure of writing some poetry to put to music for children's songs. Some of these are also included in this book of poetry. Nothing is sweeter to my ears than hearing the precious voices of children singing about Jesus.

It is with this thought that I dedicate this book to all who have inspired me: my grandmother, my family, my former students, and my friends.

Gail Frye Winter

Give Me a Noun and I'll Make You a Rhyme

"Toothpaste"

I

Squeezed

Too hard

I made

A mess

There's

Toothpaste

On my

Hands

And dress

It came

Right out

Nice and

Thin

But

It won't

Go back

In again.

"The Dragon"

There was a dragon under my bed.
He had a pointy tail and a big blue head.

He slept all day while I was at school.
At night he would come out and roar and drool.

At first I was scared when he came creeping out.
I would hide under the covers and tremble and pout.

But we became friends one night in June.
When I heard him cry a mournful tune.

He had caught his tail on a splintery old slat.
He couldn't come out and he couldn't go back.

So with my little knife and my Boy Scout book.
I cut away the splinter that had him hooked.

Now, I'm NEVER afraid when I lay down my head,
Cause nothin's gonna get me
With a dragon friend under MY bed.

"Dirt"

There's nothing I like better
Than a box full of dirt
You can do a lot of things
And never get hurt.

Add some water
Make a pie
Throw some in
Your cousin's eye

Put it in the sun
To bake
Pretend it is
A birthday cake

Sift it through
Your fingers slow
Plant a seed
Watch it grow

Put some in a
Jar with ants
Drop some down
Your brother's pants

Dig it out of
Soles of shoes
It doesn't really
Matter whose

Track it in on
Mother's floor
I wouldn't do
That anymore

So If the electricity
Goes out
And the T.V. won't work-

Just fill a box
With some
Nice brown dirt.

"Cow"

I always wanted a pony,
But Daddy bought a cow.
I wished that I could ride her,
But didn't know just how.

I got an old worn blanket,
And tossed it over her back.
I climbed the fence and jumped right on,
And gave her rump and whack.

She jumped and bawled,
And spun and reared,
I tried to hold on tight,

She tossed me high,
And flung me off,
For cows you just can't ride.

"Cheese"

Shades of creamy orange and yellow
Some with flecks of green
Some sharp and tangy
Some mild and mellow

Topped on dishes piping hot
Served sliced, cold or cubed
Served with crunchy, salty chips
Dipped in a melting pot

Small children like it-
It's soft to chew
Little brown mice and little grey mice
They like it too

These are some things
I know about cheese
Would you be so kind?
To pass me
Some please?

"Colors"

I learned to love colors,
As a small little girl,
The things all around me,
In a colorful world.

Crayons in a box,
Patches on a quilt,
Fall colors on hardwood trees,
Houses someone built.

But I have learned:

The most beautiful colors
Are the ones upon the faces,
Of all the many people
Your meet in different places.

Crayons break, quilts fade,
In winter trees are bare.
But respect, love and cherish
The colors people wear.

"Shoes"

Little to biggest
All leather shoes
Lined against the wall
I wonder whose?

First pair is tiny
The toes all rough
Someone is crawling
To make them so scuffed

Then there are sandals
Clean, white with jeweled straps
Someone is careful
And likes them like that

A basketball pair
High tops with school laces
Proud feet in those
To go with proud faces

Pink ballet slippers
Satin ribbons unfurled
Belong to a very
Growing up girl

A big, sturdy, brown boot
Has walked many miles
The wearer for sure
Gives kisses and smiles

Last pair to see
Last in the line
They look so, so tired
Those must be mine.

"Jumping"

a special milestone
when you learn how to jump

when two chubby legs
go airborne and thump

a lifetime of jumping
is about to begin

You practice and practice
all over again:

on the bed
into leaves
catch me Daddy
will you please?
off the chair
off the couch
landing with a
bump and ouch
getting bigger
swimming fine
I cand do it
jump and dive

All grown Up
Jump into Life
Take a Husband
Take a Wife

Each Jump Alone
A Leap Of Faith
One You Will Want
To Surely Take

"Imagination"

Sometimes two horses

Sometimes two cars

Sometimes a chair with two sturdy arms

It's the roots of a tall maple tree

It is all this and more

They make a fine plaything

For imagination's open door

They have grown up and out

High above the ground

They join the huge trunk

With moss all around

We fight over the biggest

My cousin and I.

"Time"

time
comes in
leaves again
has fun
snoozes some
forgets meetings
hurries greetings
comes around
slows down
begins anew
things to do
in time

Just For Students

"Mornings"

Get up, Get up, I hear my Momma say,

It's six o'clock, we've not much time.

What are you wearing to school today?

I moan, I groan, I pull the covers tight.

Oooooooooooh Umms the muffled sound I make.

Please don't turn on the light.

Slowly, so slowly I inch out of bed.

My feet touch the icy floor.

The message is sent.

It clears my sleepy head.

Yealllllllllllll!--I scream as I prance across the room.

I am awake now for real.

Better hurry really fast.

The bus will be here soon.

"Don't Call on Me"

You might not see it coming
When teacher starts to speak
She's going to call on someone
I hope it isn't me

There are things that you can do
To keep yourself from that
Put them in your brain right now
Under your thinking cap

Don't slink back in your seat
Don't hang your head down low
That's a sign you don't know "nothin"
And the guilt is sure to show
She'll call on YOU!

Don't turn around or pass a note
To get the answer true
She's got eyes that roam the room
Yup! She'll call on YOU!

Instead, wave your arms and gasp in your breath
Teachers rarely call on those
But be prepared, just in case
You're the one she chose
She'll call on YOU!

It's best to act kinda normal
But don't look her in the eye
Cause if no one else is looking
You're the one she'll try
She'll call on YOU!

For heaven's sake don't act out
Or look too dumb or smart
These are for sure "call ons"
And not for the faint of heart

If you can, make yourself
Blend in with your chair
Follow all the rules above
At best your chances are fair SHE'LL CALL ON YOU!!!!!!

"Test Day"

Their heads are bent
Their brain is spent
It's testing time today.

They say a prayer
It's just not fair
To be inside today.

They hope to pass
But if alas
They do not make the grade:

They will be ahead
Next year instead
Repeating.......I'm afraid.

Nature

"Night Concert"

Listen to the tree bugs that

Sing a crescendo song

Listen to the creek frogs that

Happily croak along

Listen to the hooty owl

Keeping perfect time

Everything together

Seems a perfect rhyme

Listen to the trees

Play percussion with the wind

Enjoy nature's concert

Played by all of these

"Dusk"

the day sky is fading
trees fade green then black
across the dusky horizon
they silhouette the sky
to the west a touch of red
whispers sun's good-by

"Magic in the Cup"

the wet earthy smell of the
mountain stream
dark brown leaves line the deep, deep creek
my cup is tin
I dip it in
I breathe the mountain water smell
I take a drink
Ah...the sweet, sweet mountain creek

"Spring Rain"

I wish I could bottle
the smell of spring rain
Words cannot describe
nothing is the same

Tis wet, but not only
something you feel
A scent that wakes the senses
wonderful and real

Things not yet touched
things not yet known
remember... remember
Beauty not yet grown

Damp nature's perfume
Sweetly scents the air
Envelopes and covers
All is lovely and fair

Winter

"Sleepy Thoughts on a Cold Winter's Night"

The sheets are cold as I slide in.
I tuck the covers under my chin.
And dream of:
Cozy rooms with roaring fires
Hats and coats lined with fur
Warming insides and hands with a mug of cocoa
A warm wiggly puppy at my feet
A fleecy robe wrapped tightly around
Or
Lying on the beach in the warm sun and sand.

"First Snow"

Hey ho, off I go

Hurrying, oh hurrying, to play in the snow

Tugging at britches and

Mittens and hats

Laughing at sister and

Calling her "Fats"

The boots are the hardest

Everyone knows

Your push and you pull

But the foot just won't go

With an:

Ooh, and an ugh, and a whump and a thump

I HATE THESE BOOTS!!

THWAMMP!!!!!!!! IT'S IN!

Golly, I'm sweating

It's time to go sledding

I move toward the door and then turn my head

"Murphy's Hill" I shout as I go

The first step is magic……CRUNCH!

In Winter's first snow.

"Christmas Magic"

Do you heat the jingle bells
Sounding on the roof?
Do you hear the tapping
Of little reindeer hoof?

There is magic in the air tonight,
Magic in the sky,
You can feel it all around,
Close your eyes and try.

Christmas is a fairy time,
Filled with awe and wonder.
Gifts of love and joyous songs,
Sent to one another.

"Ice"

Bare black limbs coated with ice
Sparkle like diamonds and shine in the eyes

Yesterday nothing but dry empty branch
Today iced with jewels that shimmer and dance

Tis wonderfully beautiful how God changes things
In the blink of an eye a splendor He brings

For Family and
All The Memories

"Baby Love"

Your baby girl
Will change your world.
She will show you things
Only "Baby Love" brings.

Chubby creases in her arms
Damp neck kisses
Bubbles on sweet pouty lips
Snug round baby in a hooded towel
A powder smell
A toothless smile
Round padded bottom to pat as you rock
Eyes shut tight, sleepy yawn
Warm scent of baby's breath
Barely there eyelashes closed in sleep
Rise and fall of napping babe

Your heart will swell.
Words cannot say.
A love so strong
Is yours today.

Enjoy your baby
Don't fret as she is grown.
For "baby love" is forever
The rarest love known.

"Blankie"

Nannie made me a blankie,
To cover little me.
Each stitch made with love,
And fashioned carefully.

What I will do with my blankie,
Is entirely up to me.
Suck on the corners, poke fingers through holes,
Or fold it over to tickle my nose.
It's my choice, you see.

I don't know what I will name it.
A few names come to mind.
La-La, Silkie, or Ho-Diappy,
I'm sure a good one I'll find.

It will be:
A name that works,
With my first words,
It's really hard to say.
I'll let you know-
When I know-
On my Blankie's naming day.

"A Builder"

My Daddy was a
Builder.
He built houses snug
And strong.
With hammers, nails,
And wood and saws,
That sing a builder's song.

The smell of fresh
Sawdust
Fills my mind with sweet
Memories,
As he sawed the boards to measure,
To fit so perfectly.

When all was done,
He'd gaze around,
Like a captain looks
Over the sea-
It needed just but
One thing more-
A happy family.

"My Cousin"

We often played together,
but we never got along.
He was mean and bratty,
I, sweet as a song.

He always pinched and hit me,
I'd cry for Mom and Dad.
"Take up for yourself," they chided.
That would make us glad.

One day we got into it.
He was pulling out my bows.
I doubled up my little fist,
And socked him in the nose.

This time it was he who went crying,
to tattle on little me.
With fearful heart I stood my ground,
proud as I could be.

"Sitting In Church"

I sat close to my Mamaw
At the church on the hill
Trying so hard
To be quiet and still

I tried not to wiggle
as I touched her soft white gloves
Occasionally hearing
Of God's grace and love

Since Momma and Daddy
both sang in the choir
I was pure comfort and love
snuggled tight beside her

Her dresses were soft
and she smelled of sweet flowers
Made sitting in church
pass many long hours

Her Bible had pages
all crinkly and thin
She lived by the Book
and the words within

Such precious memories
of us in our pew
Enveloped in love
Mamaw and me, too

"Riding My Bike"

Off with my training wheels...put on long pants
Riding a two wheeler...something I can't ....
Do just yet.......

It will be my pony
It will be my horse
Doing things together
The things I like the most

Propped against the apple tree
Deftly climb astride
Push off against the trunk just so
Off I go and ride

Wobbbbly...oh...so.....wobbbbbbly
Balance left and right
Teeter...tottttter around the drive
HOLD ON TIGHT

I Can Ride My Bike!!!!!!

Spending years together
On lazy sunfilled days
Riding toward the sunset
In childhood's dreamy haze.

"Nannie's Purse"

I wonder what is in it;

is it something old or new?

Fuzzy candy, sticky gum,

Something fun to do?

Nannie's purse is awesome.

She lets me go explore.

To find a toy or trinket

or something she has worn.

It helps me pass the time away

finding treasure in Nannie's purse.

Whether waiting at the dentist

Or sitting quietly in the church.

Sunday School Poems

"Birthday Star"

See the shining star— high in the dark blue sky
It seems to be telling
I wonder what and why

It's the birthday star,
the birthday star, beckoning, calling to wise men afar
come see the baby the blessed Birthday Boy
Born to bring the world peace and joy

Shepherds came and wise men too-
The star is calling both me and you
Come to the manger and fall on your knees
Worship sweet Jesus Who brings the world peace.

"Jubilee"

It was quiet on the hills of the Holy land
not a cloud in the starry sky
The lambs sleeping peacefully, lying at their mother's sides
It began as a hum in perfect harmony on
the cusp of something bright
When suddenly-suddenly-a song of such jubilee
Came pealing thro the clear dark night
A song of ecstasy....GLORY, GLORY Glory to God in the
highest and on earth peace good will toward men.

"Lullaby"

It's a baby in a manger sleeping sweetly, little lamb
There's His mother singing quietly, gentle fingers touch His hand
Sleep my baby, sleep dear Jesus all through
the night, dark and deep
I will always love and watch you, sleep my baby sleep.

"Hark Shepherds"

Poor little shepherd boys out in the night,
What's that ruckus**...what a fright!**
The sky once dark is all aglow, with angels singing high and low
Glory to the newborn King, Glory to the newborn King
Gather lambs let's go and see, the King of which the angels sing
We will take a baby lamb...That's the gift that we will bring.

"Camel's Song:"

Riding high upon our humps, wise men follow yonder star
Something great is happening…I hope it isn't very far
Heavy bundles in the packs, tied on carefully to our backs
Must be someone's birthday…. we think we carry gifts
A party, a party, we do not want to miss.
Chorus:
It is gold, myrrh and frankincense, gold myrrh and frankincense
Not my kind of gift but I guess it's the
thought and not the presents.

"A Fisher of Men"

Not bass or shark or even trout
That's not what my fishing is all about
I'm telling the story of Jesus you see
A fisher of men I'll be.
A fisher of men I'll be.

I'll make my mark in the soft white sand.
To show everyone just where I stand
Jesus is Lord over all the land
A fisher of men I am.
A fisher of men I am.

"Tackle Box"

I have a tackle box full of stuff
To fish for men it will be enough
Just add the story of Jesus'
And tell of the Father above

There is love, joy, and peace for bait
Kindness, goodness and then we wait...Shhh..patience

With faithfulness and gentleness the fish will bite
Add self control and we can fish all night

I have a tackle box full of stuff
To fish for men it will be enough
Just add the story about Jesus' love
And tell of the Father above

"Fishing Buddy"

I need a fishing buddy
I need a fishing friend
Jesus needs me helping
To bring the fishes in

Be my fishing buddy
Be my fishing friend
Jesus needs us helping
To bring the fishes in

I'll be your fishing buddy
I'll be your fishing friend
Jesus loves us helping
To bring the fishes in

About the Author

Gail Winter was born in Knoxville, Tennessee, and was educated at the University of Tennessee. She began writing poems during her thirty-year teaching career in the Knox County School system as a way to interest her students in poetry. This is her first publication. She has three children and eight grandchildren and lives in Knoxville with her husband, Bob.

Printed in the United States
By Bookmasters